PUBLISHED BY STUDIO PUBLICATIONS (IPSWICH) LIMITED
32 PRINCES STREET, IPSWICH, SUFFOLK, ENGLAND.

Pippa Pear is one of the Munch Bunch.

She lives in a lantern next door to her best friend, Adam Avocado.

Pippa is a very greedy pear. She eats and eats and eats and eats . . .

This morning for breakfast, she started with a big bowl of porridge.

Then she had a plate full of sausages and eggs.

And, to finish with, she was looking forward to lots of toast and honey and at least five cups of tea.

After she'd finished her big breakfast, Pippa worried in case she was getting slightly fat.

But she soon forgot about that when she thought of the big cream cake she'd made for elevenses!

Just to fill in the time before her next feed, Pippa went to see her friend, Emma Apple.

On the way, she saw Professor Peabody. He was cleaning something which looked very odd to Pippa.

"Look at these, Pippa," Peabody said. "They're genuine kitchen scales. You weigh things on them. Hop on, and we'll try them out!"

So Pippa jumped on to one side of the scales and Peabody put the weights on the other side.

"Oh that's good, Pippa. You weigh exactly the same as eleven buttons and two match-boxes."

"What!" cried Pippa. "That's terrible. Promise you'll keep it a secret. Please don't tell any of the others!"

Then she jumped off the scales and hurried away to see Emma Apple.

"Emma, Emma you must help me. I've got to go on a diet. I'm far too heavy!" cried Pippa.

Emma was so surprised, she dropped the vase of flowers she was dusting.

"Come with me, dear, we'll discuss it outside over a nice glass of water!" said Emma.

Pippa kept very still while Emma measured all round her waist.

"Mmm, I can see why you're worried. But, if you stick to this diet and do exercises with me every day, you'll soon lose that extra weight!"

"You will remember it's Top Secret, won't you?" said Pippa.

But, unknown to Emma and Pippa, Lucy Lemon had overheard their conversation. And she was looking forward to telling Suzie Celery all about it.

Pippa and Emma met the next day and did their exercises together.

They worked very hard, for over an hour, touching their toes and doing high kicks.

Afterwards, they were very tired. And Pippa was VERY hungry.

Suddenly, Suzie Celery popped up from nowhere. She was carrying a tray full of fizzy drinks and chocolate buns.

"Help yourselves, girls," she said gleefully.

But Emma gave Suzie a big glare. And she gave Pippa a dig in the side.

"Oh . . . er . . . um . . . No, thank you," said Pippa very weakly.

The next day, some of the Munch Bunch decided to go to the lake for a swim.

They were all going in Spud's car.

Except for Pippa.

She asked Olly Onion if she could borrow his bicycle. "It's such a lovely day for a bike ride," she said.

And, much to the amazement of the others, she cycled all the way there.

They were even more amazed when Pippa jumped straight in the lake, as soon as she arrived.

The others were all sunbathing and relaxing.

But Pippa was determined to swim at least twice across the lake, before she stopped for a rest.

And, while Pippa was busy swimming, Lucy and Suzie told the others about Pippa's diet.

A little while later, Pippa flopped on to the side of the lake, exhausted.

The others crowded round. They offered her hot dogs, sandwiches, cakes, bags of sweets and fizzy drinks.

But Pippa accepted only one tiny sandwich and a glass of water.

She was very miserable at having to refuse such lovely food.

The next day, Suzie and Lucy called at Pippa's house. They discovered her doing her exercises, once again.

"Are you coming with us to Sally Strawberry's tea party?" asked Suzie. "There's sure to be chocolate cake, cream meringues, and . . ."

"All right! I'll be there as soon as I've been jogging!" said Pippa quickly.

Pippa went to Sally's tea party, still wearing her track-suit and feeling very weary after her run.

Sally offered Pippa a plate full of jam tarts.

"No, thank you, Sally, a dry biscuit would be very nice. I'm not very hungry today," said Pippa, sighing to herself.

And, even when they offered her iced buns, tea cakes and fizzy drinks, Pippa still refused everything.

She was determined to stick to her diet!

It was two weeks since Pippa had started her diet. And she felt very miserable.

So she went to see Peabody to ask him to weigh her.

"Well done, Pippa," he said. "You've lost three button's worth of weight. That really is very good!"

Pippa was delighted.

Just then, Adam Avocado came along. "Well done, Pippa! Come to my house. I've got a surprise for you."

Some of the Munch Bunch had prepared a party specially for Pippa.

"We know it's been very difficult for you to diet, especially with everyone trying to tempt you," said Adam. "But we're all very proud that you have managed to stick to it for two whole weeks!"

"Well I suppose I could have just ONE day off my diet," said Pippa.

A.M.

Pippa was happier than she'd been for a long time.

"But I'll be back on that diet again tomorrow!" she said.